IEPs Made Easy: A Parent's Step-by-Step Guide to Special Education Advocacy

LETONYA F MOORE, ESQ.

Copyright © 2024 LeTonya Moore

All rights reserved.

ISBN:

DEDICATION

This book is dedicated to all of the incredible parents who trust me to advocate for their children's rights, and those who introduced me to the fantastic world of special education law.

CONTENTS

	Acknowledgments	i
1	UNDERSTANDING SPECIAL EDUCATION AND IEPS	1
2	KNOWING YOUR CHILD'S RIGHTS	7
3	PREPARING FOR YOUR CHILD'S IEP MEETING	14
4	REVIEWING AND FINALIZING THE IEP—GETTING IT RIGHT	21
5	COMMUNICATING EFFECTIVELY WITH THE IEP TEAM	28
6	MONITORING YOUR CHILD'S PROGRESS	34
7	NAVIGATING CONFLICT AND DISPUTES	40
8	NAVIGATING THE IEP MEETING: STRATEGIES FOR SUCCESS	46
9	THE IMPORTANCE OF ONGOING ADVOCACY AND SUPPORT	52
10	FOSTERING INDEPENDENCE AND SELFSUFFICIENCY	58

ACKNOWLEDGMENTS

I am deeply grateful to my parents, Patricia and Albert Moore, my son Charvez, and my sister Kathy, for their unwavering support, and to the parents who trust me to advocate for their children.

IEPs Made Easy: A Parent's Step-by-Step Guide to Special Education Advocacy

INTRODUCTION

Welcome to the World of Special Education Advocacy

As a parent of a special needs child, you already understand that the journey toward providing them with the best possible education can be overwhelming. The truth is, navigating the world of special education, particularly the Individualized Education Program (IEP) process, often feels like stepping into unfamiliar territory. If you've felt lost or powerless at any point, you are not alone. But here's the good news: by taking control of your child's IEP, you can profoundly impact their future, ensuring they receive the services, support, and opportunities they need to thrive.

This book, "IEPs Made Easy: Your Step-by-step Guide to Special Education Advocacy," is designed with you in mind. Whether you're just beginning your advocacy journey, or you've been in the system for years, this guide will empower you to become the most effective advocate for your child's unique needs. The feeling of confusion and frustration can be replaced by clarity, confidence, and a sense of control. Imagine walking into every IEP meeting with a deep understanding of the process and the unwavering belief that you can ensure the best possible outcome for your child. This transformation is within your reach.

Why Advocacy Matters: The Key to Unlocking Your Child's Potential

At the heart of this journey is one powerful truth: you are your child's best advocate. No one understands your child's strengths, challenges, and needs better than you. When you embrace this role and take intentional steps to actively engage in the IEP process, you can unlock doors that might otherwise remain closed. It is not just about fighting for the services your child is entitled to; it's about creating an environment where your child can flourish and achieve their full potential.

You may have encountered educators, administrators, or specialists who seem like experts, but always remember that you are the expert on your child. In fact, research shows that parents who take an active role in their child's education see more positive outcomes, both academically and socially. By equipping yourself with the right tools and strategies, you can ensure that your voice is heard, respected, and acted upon.

The Power of Knowing the System: Turning Fear into Confidence

The IEP process can feel intimidating because it's filled with legal jargon, technical terms, and formal procedures. But what if, instead of feeling overwhelmed by this complexity, you could approach it with calm confidence?

Neurolinguistic Programming (NLP) teaches us that the language we use—both in our minds and in conversation—shapes our reality. Right now, you might be telling yourself, "This is too complicated for me," or "I don't know how to fight for what my child needs." But imagine the shift if you told yourself, "I am capable of understanding this," or "I have the power to advocate successfully for my child."

This guide will help you reframe your thoughts and feelings about the IEP process. You'll learn not only the practical steps but also powerful mindset techniques that can dramatically change your experience as an advocate. By transforming your inner dialogue and using positive, action-oriented language, you will notice an increase in your effectiveness as a parent advocate.

A Step-by-step Roadmap to Success

This book breaks the IEP process down into manageable, easy to follow steps so you can feel fully prepared at each stage. We'll start by exploring what special education is, what an IEP entails, and why it matters. Then, we'll walk you through each phase of the process, from requesting an evaluation to preparing for your first IEP meeting, to ensuring your child's IEP goals are specific and measurable. You'll also learn how to track your child's progress, how to handle disagreements with the school team, and how to adjust your child's plan as their needs evolve over time.

In addition to practical guidance, this book will also introduce you to simple, effective NLP techniques that will help you communicate with confidence, remain calm during challenging situations, and ultimately advocate for your child in the most powerful way possible. By blending strategy with mindset mastery, you'll be able to tackle each meeting and decision with clarity and purpose.

The Journey Ahead: Empowering Yourself and Your Child

As you work through the chapters of this book, you'll notice a powerful transformation happening within yourself. Each step forward brings you closer to a place where you no longer feel like an outsider in the special education system. Instead, you'll become a true partner in your child's educational journey—someone who can engage confidently with teachers, specialists, and administrators to ensure your child's needs are met.

It is time to stop worrying about what might go wrong and

IEPs Made Easy: A Parent's Step-by-Step Guide to Special Education Advocacy

start focusing on what can go right. Every step you take as your child's advocate is a step toward their brighter future. Together, we will make the IEP process not just manageable, but empowering—for both you and your child. Your advocacy, combined with a structured, well-informed approach, will become the key to unlocking your child's potential and ensuring they receive the education they deserve.

So, let's begin this journey together. You are capable. You are powerful. You are your child's strongest ally. And by the end of this guide, the IEP process will feel easy, straightforward, and, most importantly, effective in supporting your child's unique educational needs.

1

UNDERSTANDING SPECIAL EDUCATION AND IEPS

Before you can advocate effectively for your child, it's essential to have a solid understanding of the special education system and, specifically, the Individualized Education Program (IEP). The more familiar you are with the terminology, laws, and processes involved, the more confident and empowered you'll feel at every step of the way. Remember, knowledge is power, and the more you know, the stronger your voice will become in advocating for your child.

In this chapter, we're going to break down the fundamentals of special education, clarify what an IEP really is, and why it's so critical for your child's success. By the end of this chapter, you'll not only understand the basics but will start to feel that "I've got this!" attitude you need as you move forward.

What is Special Education?

Let's start at the beginning. Special education refers to the tailormade educational services designed to meet the unique needs of students with disabilities. These services ensure that your child can access the same educational opportunities as their peers, despite the challenges they may face. Imagine this as building a custom bridge over the gaps your child may have—bridges that allow them to access the learning and support they need to succeed.

Special education isn't a "one size fits all" solution, and that's what makes it so powerful. Your child's educational experience should be as unique as they are, designed to target their specific strengths and areas of need. The key is that your child is entitled to this by law, not just as a favor or courtesy. It's essential to recognize that the services available are designed to help your child thrive, and you are their strongest advocate in making sure those services are appropriately provided.

Let's look at an example. I once worked with a family whose child, a bright and curious second grader, was struggling with reading and attention issues. His teachers had recommended extra help, but without a formal IEP in place, he wasn't receiving the individualized support he really needed. Once we helped the parents navigate the IEP process, the school provided specialized reading interventions and classroom accommodations tailored to his learning style. The change was incredible: not only did his reading improve, but his self-esteem soared. This is what's possible when you understand and advocate for the right services.

Key Terms You Need to Know

As you begin to navigate this world, you'll encounter various terms that might feel overwhelming at first. Don't worry—you don't have to memorize everything at once. Instead, let's focus on some key concepts that will be most helpful as you move forward.

IEP (Individualized Education Program): This is a legally binding document that outlines the specific educational goals, services, and accommodations that your child will receive. More on this in a bit.

IDEA (Individuals with Disabilities Education Act): This is the federal law that guarantees all children with disabilities the right to a free appropriate public education (FAPE). Understanding IDEA is crucial because it forms the foundation of your child's rights in special education.

FAPE (Free Appropriate Public Education): Your child has the right to receive an education that meets their individual needs at no cost to you. This isn't just about getting any education—it's about making sure the education your child receives is appropriate and tailored to their unique challenges and strengths.

LRE (Least Restrictive Environment): This term refers to the requirement that your child be educated in the most inclusive setting possible, meaning they should be placed in a regular classroom with peers whenever appropriate. Your child has the right to be part of the general education setting as much as possible.

Don't let these terms overwhelm you. We will revisit them throughout this book, and each time they will become clearer, adding another layer of confidence to your role as an advocate.

What is an IEP?

Now, let's get to the heart of the matter: the Individualized Education Program (IEP). Think of the IEP as your child's educational road map. It's not just a document filled with technical jargon; it's a powerful tool that charts a course for your child's educational success.

An IEP is developed by a team that includes you (the

parent), your child's teachers, and other professionals like school psychologists or speech therapists, depending on your child's needs. It outlines your child's specific goals, services they will receive, and any accommodations or modifications that will help them access the curriculum. In short, it's your child's personalized learning plan.

Here's an example of how an IEP can make a world of difference. I worked with a family whose child, a middle school student with ADHD, was constantly falling behind due to disorganization and difficulty focusing on class. Before they had an IEP, the school viewed his challenges as behavioral issues rather than educational ones. Once the parents advocated for an IEP, we helped them secure accommodations like extended time on tests, a modified homework schedule, and regular check-ins with a guidance counselor. These simple but targeted adjustments allowed him to excel academically and reduced the frustration he had previously felt. The power of a well-crafted IEP cannot be overstated.

The Legal Foundation of IEPs: IDEA

The IEP process is more than just a series of meetings and paperwork—it's a legal right. Under the Individuals with Disabilities Education Act (IDEA), every child with a disability is entitled to an education that meets their unique needs. This is not optional for schools. They are legally required to provide your child with a Free Appropriate Public Education (FAPE), and the IEP is the way to ensure that happens.

Understanding IDEA gives you leverage as an advocate. When you know the law is on your side, it changes how you approach the process. Instead of feeling like you're asking for favors, you realize you're asserting your child's rights.

Imagine walking into an IEP meeting, not just as a parent, but as an informed advocate with the law backing you up. This mindset shift alone can significantly change the outcome of the meeting.

Why Every Child Needs a Well-Crafted IEP

Every child with special needs is unique, which is why every IEP should be too. The IEP serves as both a shield and a sword. It shields your child from being overlooked or misunderstood by ensuring their needs are formally recognized and addressed. And it's a sword in that it empowers you to demand the specific services and supports that will help your child succeed. A well-crafted IEP isn't just a formality; it's a game changer.

I've seen students who, without an IEP, were misunderstood, isolated, and left to struggle. But with a comprehensive, individualized IEP, those same students received the attention and support they deserved. Their educational experience was transformed because their parents took the time to advocate for an IEP that truly reflected their child's needs.

For example, a student with a reading disability who was once labeled as "lazy" or "unmotivated" had an entirely different experience once his IEP included specialized reading instruction and assistive technology. Suddenly, his teachers saw his potential, and his grades improved. This is the kind of transformation that's possible when the IEP is written with care and precision.

Conclusion: The Power is in Your Hands

By now, you understand that an IEP is not just a bureaucratic requirement—it's the key to unlocking your child's potential. And here's the most important takeaway: you have the power to ensure that this key is used effectively.

As you move forward, remember that every piece of knowledge you gain strengthens your ability to advocate for your child. You're no longer on the sidelines, unsure of how to help. Instead, you're stepping into the role of a confident, informed advocate who knows that you are your child's best and most powerful voice.

In the chapters ahead, we'll dive deeper into how you can make this process work for your child. But for now, take a deep breath and know that you've already taken the first step toward creating an educational environment where your child can thrive. You are not alone in this journey—and together, we will make sure that IEPs truly are made easy.

2

KNOWING YOUR CHILD'S RIGHTS

Now that you have a foundational understanding of what an IEP is and why it matters, it's time to dive into something even more powerful: your child's rights. This chapter will empower you to step into meetings, discussions, and any advocacy situation with absolute confidence. When you understand your child's rights—*and how to assert them*—you move from feeling like an outsider to being a key player in your child's education. You are not just asking for what your child needs; you are ensuring that the law protects those needs.

As we explore the key laws that govern special education and your role as a parent, you'll discover just how much power you have. Knowing these rights gives you leverage, and more importantly, it gives your child the opportunity to thrive.

Understanding Federal Laws: IDEA, Section 504, and ADA

To start, let's look at the three main federal laws that provide the foundation for your child's rights: IDEA (Individuals with Disabilities Education Act), Section 504 of the Rehabilitation Act, and the Americans with Disabilities Act (ADA). Each of these laws serves a unique purpose, but they all work together to ensure that children with disabilities receive the education they deserve.

IEPs Made Easy: A Parent's Step-by-Step Guide to Special Education Advocacy

#1. IDEA: The Backbone of Special Education

The Individuals with Disabilities Education Act (IDEA) is the cornerstone of special education law in the United States. This law guarantees that every child with a disability has the right to a Free Appropriate Public Education (FAPE). It's what ensures that your child will not only receive an education but that the education will meet their unique needs.

Here's where your power lies: the law requires schools to provide individualized services. Schools aren't allowed to offer a generic program or fit your child into a "one size fits all" system. Instead, they must design a program specifically for your child based on their strengths, needs, and learning style. This is the foundation for the IEP process, and it gives you a legal platform to stand on when advocating for your child.

Let me give you an example. I once worked with a family whose child had a speech delay. The school initially offered group speech therapy once a week, which wasn't enough to address the child's needs. After we reminded the school of their obligation under IDEA, the IEP team agreed to provide one-on-one sessions, which dramatically improved the child's progress. This is the kind of advocacy that understanding IDEA makes possible.

#2. Section 504: Protecting Access and Accommodations

Section 504 of the Rehabilitation Act goes hand in hand with IDEA but has a broader scope. While IDEA applies specifically to children who need special education services, Section 504 protects the rights of any individual with a disability, ensuring they have equal access to all school programs and activities.

Even if your child doesn't qualify for an IEP under IDEA, they may still be entitled to accommodations under a 504 Plan. This could include things like extended time on tests, preferential seating, or access to assistive technology. Section 504 ensures that no child is left behind simply because they need a little extra support.

#3. ADA: Eliminating Barriers

The Americans with Disabilities Act (ADA) is a civil rights law that goes beyond the school system to ensure that individuals with disabilities are not discriminated against in any area of public life. While it's not specific to education, it plays an important role in ensuring that schools provide an accessible and inclusive environment.

For example, if your child uses a wheelchair, the ADA requires the school to provide accessible facilities, such as ramps or elevators. If your child has a visual impairment, the ADA ensures that materials are provided in formats they can access, such as Braille or audio recordings. The ADA is another powerful tool that ensures your child can fully participate in their education, free from barriers.

Parental Rights and Responsibilities

Now that you understand the laws protecting your child, let's shift focus to your rights as a parent. You are not a passive participant in this process—you are a central figure, and your voice carries weight. You have a set of legally defined rights and responsibilities that enable you to be a powerful advocate for your child's education.

IEPs Made Easy: A Parent's Step-by-Step Guide to Special Education Advocacy

#1. Your Right to Participate in the IEP Process

The law is clear: you have the right to be involved in every step of your child's IEP process. This means you have the right to attend all IEP meetings, to contribute to discussions, and to help shape the goals and services in the IEP. You also have the right to bring in experts or advocates to support you during these meetings.

Don't ever let a school or district make you feel like you're just there to listen. You are there to contribute—and your input is invaluable because no one knows your child better than you do.

#2. Your Right to Request an Evaluation

If you believe your child needs special education services, you have the right to request a formal evaluation from the school. The school cannot deny this request without a valid reason, and they are required by law to conduct the evaluation within a specific timeframe. If the evaluation shows that your child qualifies for special education services, the school must develop an IEP to meet those needs.

#3. Your Right to Disagree

One of the most powerful rights you have is the right to disagree. If you don't agree with the evaluation results, the proposed IEP, or the services the school is offering, you have the right to challenge those decisions. You do not have to accept anything less than what your child deserves.

This can be intimidating for some parents, but remember you are asserting your child's rights, not asking for favors. In one case, I helped a family whose child was initially denied speech therapy services. The school's evaluation concluded that the child didn't qualify, but we knew better. The parents requested an independent evaluation, which proved the need for services, and the school was legally required to provide them. This is the power of knowing your rights.

Understanding Procedural Safeguards and Due Process

Alongside your rights as a parent are procedural safeguards—legal protections that ensure you have a fair say in your child's education. These safeguards are designed to protect both you and your child, ensuring that schools comply with the law and that your child's educational needs are being met.

#1. Procedural Safeguards Notice

The Procedural Safeguards Notice is a document that the school is required to provide you at least once a year or whenever a significant decision is made regarding your child's IEP. This document outlines all your legal rights, including your right to be involved in the process, to receive written notice of any changes to your child's services, and to resolve disputes.

It's important to review this document carefully. If you're unsure about anything, don't hesitate to ask questions or seek outside support. This is your child's education we're talking about, and there's no such thing as being too informed.

#2. Resolving Disagreements: Mediation and Due Process

If you and the school can't agree on your child's services, there are formal processes in place to resolve disputes.

Mediation is a voluntary process where an impartial mediator helps you and the school reach an agreement. It's often a good first step because it can resolve issues without going to court.

However, if mediation doesn't work, you have the right to request a due process hearing. This is a more formal legal proceeding where you present your case before an impartial hearing officer. While due process can seem daunting, it is your ultimate safeguard if the school is failing to meet your child's needs.

One family I worked with used due process after their school district refused to provide occupational therapy services for their child, even though the IEP clearly stated it was necessary. Through due process, we were able to secure those services, ensuring the child received the support they needed. Due process is a powerful tool—don't be afraid to use it if you need to.

Conclusion: You Are Empowered

By understanding your child's rights and your role in the special education process, you are already more empowered than most parents. You know the laws that protect your child, and you know how to assert those rights with confidence. You are no longer just a participant in your child's education—you are the advocate that can make real change happen.

As you continue on this journey, remember you have the knowledge, the power, and the legal backing to ensure your child gets the education they deserve. With each new piece of information, you grow stronger and more capable. This confidence, combined with your love and determination, makes you the most important person in your child's education. Keep moving forward—you're on the right path.

In the next chapter, we'll explore the first critical steps in getting your child's IEP process started, from requesting evaluations to preparing for the first IEP meeting. You've got this—and we're here to help every step of the way.

3

PREPARING FOR YOUR CHILD'S IEP MEETING

By this point, you're armed with knowledge about the special education process and your child's legal rights. You understand the power of an IEP and the importance of advocating for your child. Now, it's time to put that knowledge into action—by preparing for the all-important IEP meeting. This chapter will guide you through each step of the preparation process, so you walk into the meeting feeling confident and ready to advocate for your child's unique needs.

However, while we'll cover the preparation process in detail, it's important to understand that navigating the complexities of these meetings is not always straightforward. Parents often start with the best intentions and plenty of confidence but quickly realize just how complex the system can be. Sometimes, things get overwhelming, and that's when many parents have turned to us for help—and that's perfectly okay.

Let's explore what you can expect and how to approach the meeting, so you can decide the best way to move forward.

Step 1: Know the Players in the Room

When you first walk into an IEP meeting, you might feel

a bit outnumbered. In addition to you and your child (if appropriate), there will be several school staff members present. The makeup of the IEP team typically includes:

General Education Teacher: If your child participates in the general education classroom, this teacher will provide insights into how your child is functioning in a regular class setting.
Special Education Teacher: This individual works with your child and understands their specific learning challenges and strengths.
School Administrator: Usually a principal or vice principal, this person has the authority to allocate resources and approve services.
School Psychologist or Other Specialists: Depending on your child's needs, specialists such as a speech therapist, occupational therapist, or school psychologist may be involved.
IEP Coordinator: This person ensures that the meeting follows legal guidelines and facilitates the discussion.

As you prepare for the meeting, familiarize yourself with the roles of each participant. When you know who will be in the room, it's easier to stay focused and contribute meaningfully to the conversation. Remember, you belong at that table. It's important to stay grounded and confident in your understanding of your child's needs.

However, it's also helpful to acknowledge that these professionals bring expertise in areas that may be unfamiliar to you. They know the education system inside and out, while you may only be experiencing it for the first time. Many parents walk into their first IEP meeting thinking they'll be fine, only to feel overwhelmed by the sheer volume of information and professional jargon being thrown their way. In some cases, parents found themselves nodding along without fully understanding what was being discussed—and later realized that critical decisions had been made without their full input.

Step 2: Gathering and Organizing Key Information

You know your child better than anyone else, and that's a powerful advantage. Before the meeting, it's crucial to gather all relevant information about your child's needs, strengths, and challenges. This can include:

Medical reports or evaluations: If your child has been evaluated by outside professionals (such as developmental pediatricians, psychologists, or therapists), bring copies of those reports.

Previous school reports: Include any past evaluations or progress reports from the school.

Samples of your child's work: Sometimes, showing specific examples of your child's work can provide valuable insight into their progress or struggles.

One parent I worked with had initially prepared for her son's IEP meeting by collecting all his schoolwork and writing down her own observations. While this was a great first step, she soon found that the school team's technical explanations and formal reports were hard to interpret. During the meeting, the discussion veered toward topics she hadn't anticipated, and she felt out of her depth. After seeking help from a special education advocate, she realized she needed to fully understand the school's assessments before stepping into the next meeting.

This is a common experience. Parents are often thrown off by unexpected assessments or by reports that don't align with what they see at home. While you may feel fully prepared with your own insights, it's important to also understand how the school measures your child's progress and needs.

In our experience, parents feel much more confident when they partner with someone who can help them break down the school's reports and ensure they're fully aligned with what's best for their child.

Step 3: Setting Clear Goals and Priorities

One of the most important parts of the IEP meeting is setting goals for your child's academic and personal development. These goals will guide the services and accommodations provided, so it's crucial that they reflect your child's true needs.

Before the meeting, think about your child's current performance and what they should realistically achieve within the next year. For example, if your child has difficulty reading, a goal might be to increase their reading comprehension by a certain level. Or, if your child struggles with social skills, a goal could be to improve their ability to interact with peers in structured settings.

It can be tempting to leave goalsetting to the experts in the room, but you have valuable insight into what your child truly needs. However, the process of creating specific, measurable goals can be tricky. One mother, for instance, wanted her daughter to improve her math skills and trusted the school to set the right goals. But when she reviewed the IEP later, she realized the goals were vague, and the supports weren't strong enough. Eventually, she reached out to us for help in revising the IEP. After we worked together, the new goals were clear and measurable, which allowed her daughter to make meaningful progress.

IEPs Made Easy: A Parent's Step-by-Step Guide to Special Education Advocacy

You know your child's potential, but sometimes translating that into specific goals requires a little extra support. The more defined the goals, the easier it is to hold the school accountable for achieving them—and that's where we can help.

Step 4: Navigating the Meeting with Confidence

When you step into the IEP meeting, you should feel prepared and ready to advocate for your child. But, as we've mentioned before, these meetings can quickly become overwhelming. You might be introduced to unfamiliar terms like SMART goals (Specific, Measurable, Achievable, Relevant, Timebound) or FAPE (Free Appropriate Public Education). You may also be confronted with professionals who seem to know the system much better than you do.

It's in these moments that some parents start to feel like they're losing control of the conversation. In one case, a parent I worked with started off feeling confident in the meeting, only to realize halfway through that the school team was making decisions about services that didn't feel right. By the time she fully understood what was happening, the meeting had ended, and she felt like she hadn't effectively advocated for her child. She came to us for support in revisiting those decisions and making sure her child's IEP was adjusted appropriately.

This doesn't have to happen to you. While you can absolutely be a strong advocate for your child, having a team behind you to navigate the nuances of these meetings can make all the difference. Our role is to ensure that your voice is heard and that your child's IEP truly reflects their needs.

Step 5: Knowing When to Ask for Help

It's important to acknowledge that special education advocacy is complex. The professionals at the IEP meeting have years of experience working within this system, and as a parent, you may only be encountering it for the first time. It's completely natural to feel unsure or overwhelmed at points in the process.

Many parents begin by trying to handle everything themselves. They attend the meetings, ask questions, and advocate to the best of their ability. But at a certain point, they often realize they need help. One parent I worked with attended several meetings before realizing that despite her best efforts, the school wasn't providing the necessary services. When she brought us in, we were able to advocate on her behalf, and within a few weeks, her child was receiving the support they needed.

Don't wait until you feel completely lost or frustrated. It's okay to recognize when professional support can make the difference between an adequate IEP and one that fully meets your child's potential. Remember, you are your child's strongest advocate, but you don't have to do it alone.

Conclusion: Empowerment Through Preparation

By preparing for your IEP meeting thoughtfully and thoroughly, you are taking an essential step toward securing the services your child needs. You've already gained so much knowledge about your child's rights and the IEP process, and now you're ready to put it into practice. But remember, you don't have to navigate these waters entirely by yourself.

IEPs Made Easy: A Parent's Step-by-Step Guide to Special Education Advocacy

Just as every child is unique, so is every IEP meeting. As you go through this process, recognize that it's okay to seek support when needed. Our team is here to ensure that your child's IEP is comprehensive, actionable, and tailored to their success.

In the next chapter, we'll explore how to review and finalize the IEP, making sure it truly reflects your child's needs and setting them on the path to success. You're doing an amazing job so far, and with each step, you're getting closer to achieving the best possible outcome for your child. You've got this—together, we can make sure your child's future is as bright as it should be.

4

REVIEWING AND FINALIZING THE IEP—GETTING IT RIGHT

You've done the research, gathered all the necessary information, and participated in your child's IEP meeting. Now comes a critical moment in your advocacy journey: reviewing and finalizing the IEP document. This is the final step before your child's individualized plan is put into action, and it's one of the most important stages. This is where you ensure that everything is aligned with your child's unique needs.

While this step can be exciting, it can also be a bit overwhelming. Many parents initially feel confident reviewing the IEP on their own, but when they start diving into the details, they often realize that the language is highly technical, and they aren't sure how to spot potential gaps or issues. You're not alone if you feel this way—many parents have been right where you are now. In fact, we've had countless families come to us after attempting to finalize their child's IEP independently, only to find that they needed guidance to make sure nothing was overlooked.

In this chapter, we'll guide you through the key steps to reviewing and finalizing the IEP, empowering you with knowledge while highlighting when you may need a little extra support to get everything just right.

IEPs Made Easy: A Parent's Step-by-Step Guide to Special Education Advocacy

Step 1: Carefully Review the IEP Goals and Services

The goals outlined in your child's IEP are the foundation for their educational success. These goals should be specific, measurable, and tailored to address your child's academic, social, emotional, or behavioral challenges. You want to ensure that the goals reflect your child's true potential, but achieving this balance isn't always easy. The language in the IEP can sometimes be vague, and it's important to make sure the goals are clear enough to hold the school accountable.

For example, a parent we worked with thought her child's IEP goals were appropriate because they seemed well written at first glance. However, upon closer review, she realized the goals weren't specific enough, making it hard to track progress. The IEP stated that her child would "improve reading comprehension," but it didn't outline how much improvement was expected or what supports would be put in place to help achieve that goal.

After working with us, we revised the goal to specify that her child would increase reading comprehension by one grade level in six months, with 1:1 reading instruction twice a week. That level of specificity made all the difference, and the school was able to deliver services that led to real progress.

When reviewing your child's IEP, ask yourself: Are these goals specific and measurable? Do they reflect my child's true needs? Are the services being offered sufficient to help meet those goals?

If you're unsure about any part of the goals or services, that's a red flag. It's completely understandable if you're feeling overwhelmed at this stage, but you don't have to do it alone. That's where our experience comes in—we help parents translate those goals into real, tangible outcomes, ensuring that the IEP is as strong as possible.

Step 2: Watch for Red Flags in the Language

The language used in the IEP is another key area where things can get tricky. Educational jargon can make it difficult to fully understand what services your child is actually receiving. This is where many parents get tripped up—they start reading through the IEP, only to find that terms like "least restrictive environment" or "related services" are used, but it's unclear how those will play out day to day.

One parent we worked with found herself in this exact situation. Her child's IEP mentioned that he would be placed in the "least restrictive environment," but there was no detail on what that meant in practice. Did it mean he would spend most of the day in a general education classroom? Would there be an aide? She wasn't sure, and that ambiguity led to confusion when her child wasn't receiving the support she expected.

We stepped in to clarify what was missing and helped her request an amendment that outlined specific details. We ensured the IEP clearly stated the number of hours per week her child would be in a general education setting, along with the exact level of support provided by a special education teacher. This small change made a world of difference for both her and her child, and it's exactly the kind of detail you need to look for when reviewing the language of your child's IEP.

As you read through the document, remember vague language is not your friend. If you come across terms that seem unclear or overly broad, ask questions until you get clarity. And if you're feeling unsure about how to interpret the language, that's when reaching out for professional support can save you from future frustration.

Step 3: Understanding the Service Matrix

Once the goals and services are clearly outlined, the next step is understanding how those services will be delivered. This is often referred to as the service matrix or schedule of services. This part of the IEP lays out exactly how much time your child will spend receiving special education services, whether that's in a resource room, general classroom, or in the form of therapies like speech or occupational therapy.

It can be easy to miss important details here, especially if you're not used to reading educational documents. Many parents assume that their child will receive services every day or in a certain setting, only to find out later that it's far less frequent than they expected.

One mother I worked with was surprised to learn that her child's speech therapy was only scheduled for 15 minutes a week, even though the IEP had mentioned "speech therapy support." She thought that meant her child would receive much more substantial help. After she hired us, we were able to advocate for an increase in speech therapy to twice a week for 30 minutes, ensuring her child received the right level of service.

This is a common pitfall. The way services are structured in the IEP can sometimes look comprehensive, but in reality, they may not be enough. As you review the IEP, make sure the service schedule reflects the support your child needs. If you feel unsure about what's appropriate for your child, that's where we can step in to help you navigate the complexities.

Step 4: Clarifying Accommodations and Modifications

Accommodations and modifications are key components of your child's IEP. Accommodations are changes in how your child is taught or tested, while modifications are changes to what your child is expected to learn. For example, an accommodation might be providing extra time on tests, while a modification might involve simplifying the test material.

While these terms sound straightforward, they often get confused—even by school staff. We've seen cases where parents thought their child was receiving the right accommodations, only to discover that they weren't being implemented as expected. One father came to us after realizing that, despite the IEP specifying extra time for tests, his son was still being rushed through exams, leading to unnecessary frustration.

We helped him work with the school to ensure the accommodations were followed to the letter, and his son's performance improved as a result. It's crucial to verify that accommodations are not just listed on paper, but actually implemented in the classroom.

As you finalize the IEP, ask specific questions about how accommodations will be delivered. If you're not sure if the accommodations or modifications are right for your child, consider seeking expert advice to make sure nothing is left to chance.

Step 5: Knowing When to Call in Reinforcements.

IEPs Made Easy: A Parent's Step-by-Step Guide to Special Education Advocacy

Reviewing the IEP is a big responsibility. You want to get it right, and the stakes are high—this document will guide your child's education for the next year. If you're feeling confident, that's great! But if you're feeling a bit unsure or overwhelmed, know that it's completely normal to ask for help at this stage. Many parents start off feeling like they can handle everything themselves, only to realize later that the IEP was missing key details or that certain services weren't being delivered as expected.

One parent we worked with felt that the IEP meeting had gone well, and she felt good about the plan that was in place. However, when the school year started, she noticed her child wasn't making the expected progress, and she began to worry that the IEP wasn't being fully followed. After reaching out to us, we reviewed the IEP in detail and discovered that several services were listed vaguely, leading to confusion about how they were supposed to be delivered. We were able to clarify the language and ensure her child received the full level of support.

This is not uncommon—sometimes parents don't realize the importance of certain details until later. That's why it's so important to have a team behind you who can help ensure every part of the IEP is clear and actionable from the start.

Conclusion: Don't Leave Anything to Chance

Finalizing your child's IEP is one of the most important steps you'll take as their advocate. You have the power to make sure this document truly reflects your child's needs. But remember, it's okay to feel overwhelmed or unsure. Many parents have been exactly where you are now ready to advocate for their child, but uncertain about the technicalities and nuances of the process.

If you've reviewed the IEP and everything looks solid, fantastic! You're well on your way to securing the services your child needs. But if you've started to feel like there are details that don't add up or services that seem unclear, it's a good time to call in reinforcements. That's where we come in—to help you review, clarify, and ensure that your child's IEP is airtight.

PARENT IEP SUCCESS TIP: We never advise parents to sign the IEP at the meeting. Why? You have just been in the meeting, and you do not have time to digest everything. Also, some districts will tell you that signing is only for participation and they have you sign in both places, participation and agreement. Beware of this tactic.

The next chapter will explore what happens once the IEP is finalized and put into action. We'll cover how to track your child's progress and what to do if things aren't being done properly.

5

COMMUNICATING EFFECTIVELY WITH THE IEP TEAM

Now that you've reviewed and finalized your child's Individualized Education Program (IEP), it's time to discuss one of the most crucial aspects of ensuring its success: communication with the IEP team. Effective communication will enable you to maintain a collaborative relationship with school personnel and advocate for your child's needs more successfully.

While you may feel equipped with knowledge and tools to advocate for your child, navigating conversations with experienced professionals can sometimes be daunting. Many parents have found themselves overwhelmed during IEP discussions, unsure of how to articulate their thoughts or address the school's input. Recognizing that these conversations can feel intimidating is important, but with the right strategies, you can find your voice and effectively communicate your child's needs.

Let's explore how to communicate effectively with the IEP team, ensuring that you remain an empowered advocate for your child.

IEPs Made Easy: A Parent's Step-by-Step Guide to Special Education Advocacy

Step 1: Establishing Open Lines of Communication

To create a successful partnership with the IEP team, it's essential to establish open lines of communication. This begins with being proactive in reaching out to school staff before and after meetings. Here's how you can foster effective communication:

Initiate Contact: Don't wait until the next IEP meeting to voice your thoughts or concerns. Send an email or make a phone call to discuss any pressing issues. The more familiar you become with the IEP team, the more comfortable you will feel expressing your ideas.

Ask Questions: If you're uncertain about any part of your child's IEP, don't hesitate to ask questions. School personnel are there to help, and they appreciate when parents take an active role in their child's education.

One parent I worked with initially felt hesitant to reach out to the special education teacher. She was worried that her questions might seem trivial or that she might come off as uninformed. However, when she finally mustered the courage to send an email, she was pleasantly surprised by the teacher's willingness to engage. Together, they discussed her child's progress and potential strategies for improvement. This parent's experience shows that establishing communication with the IEP team is not only beneficial but also achievable.

Step 2: Using Clear and Concise Language

When communicating with the IEP team, clarity is key. School personnel often use technical jargon that can feel overwhelming. To ensure your concerns and needs are understood, it's important to express your thoughts clearly and concisely. Here are some tips:

Be Specific: Instead of general statements like "my child struggles in school," provide specific examples, such as "my child finds it difficult to complete math assignments independently." This helps the team understand exactly what you're observing.

Use 'I' Statements: Frame your concerns using "I" statements to express your thoughts without sounding accusatory. For instance, say "I feel that my child would benefit from additional reading support" rather than "The school isn't providing enough help."

A mother I supported tried to address her son's challenges in the classroom during the IEP meeting. Initially, she expressed her feelings vaguely, saying she was concerned about his overall performance. However, as she continued to struggle to articulate her thoughts, the meeting shifted focus to what the school felt was adequate support. Afterward, she realized that her approach lacked clarity and specificity. She turned to our team for guidance, and together we helped her reframe her concerns in a way that clearly conveyed her son's specific needs. With this newfound confidence, she was able to advocate effectively in future meetings.

Step 3: Documenting Conversations and Agreements

Keeping a record of all communication with the IEP team is essential. Documentation not only helps you track your child's progress but also provides a reference point for discussions. Here's how to approach documentation:

Take Notes: During meetings and phone calls, take detailed notes on what was discussed, decisions made, and any agreements reached. This will ensure you have a clear understanding of what to expect moving forward.

Summarize Follow Up Actions: After meetings, consider sending a brief email summarizing the discussion and any agreed upon actions. This creates a record that everyone can refer to, reducing misunderstandings.

For example, one father attempted to manage his child's IEP communication alone and found it challenging to keep track of all the details. After a few meetings, he realized he couldn't remember everything that was discussed, and as a result, he felt unprepared for follow-ups. After reaching out to our team, he learned how to document conversations effectively. By summarizing discussions and maintaining a clear record, he was able to confidently approach subsequent meetings. This simple change empowered him to stay engaged and informed.

Step 4: Building Positive Relationships

While advocating for your child's needs is essential, remember that the IEP team members are also professionals who care about student success. Building positive relationships can go a long way in creating a collaborative atmosphere. Here's how to foster those relationships:

Express Gratitude: Acknowledge the hard work that educators and specialists put into their jobs. A simple "thank you" can foster goodwill and encourage a positive relationship.

Engage in Collaboration: Rather than approaching meetings with a confrontational mindset, frame discussions as collaborative efforts. For instance, say, "I believe we all want what's best for my child, and I'd love to work together to find solutions."

A parent I worked with initially approached the IEP meetings with skepticism. She felt the school team was more focused on compliance than genuinely supporting her child. However, when she began expressing appreciation for their efforts, she noticed a shift in the dynamics of the meetings. The team became more open to her suggestions, and together they developed a more robust plan for her child. This transformation highlights how positivity can strengthen communication and collaboration.

Step 5: Knowing When to Seek Support

As you navigate the communication process, it's essential to recognize that it's perfectly okay to seek additional support when you feel overwhelmed. You may find yourself in situations where discussions become complex, or you feel unsure of your rights.

When parents initially attempt to handle all aspects of the IEP process themselves, it can lead to feelings of inadequacy. One mother I supported was determined to advocate for her child's needs but quickly became frustrated by the educational jargon and the intricacies of the IEP. She tried her best to handle everything alone, but the more she struggled, the more overwhelmed she felt. Ultimately, she reached out to our team for guidance.

With our support, she was able to focus her energy on what truly mattered—her child's needs—while we handled the complexities of communication and advocacy. This allowed her to regain her confidence and approach meetings with a clearer mindset, knowing she had a team backing her up.

Conclusion: Embracing Your Role as Advocate

Effective communication with the IEP team is vital for your child's success. By establishing open lines of communication, using clear language, documenting conversations, building positive relationships, and knowing when to seek support, you can navigate this process with confidence.

While it's normal to feel out of your league when dealing with experienced professionals, remember that you possess invaluable insights about your child. Your voice matters, and by honing your communication skills, you can ensure that your child's needs are heard and addressed.

In the next chapter, we will explore how to monitor your child's progress throughout the year, equipping you with strategies to ensure that the IEP remains a living document that continues to support your child's growth and development. You are on a journey toward success, and each step you take brings you closer to securing the educational experience your child deserves.

6

MONITORING YOUR CHILD'S PROGRESS

Congratulations! You have reached a pivotal chapter in your journey as an advocate for your child with special needs. Now that you have a well crafted Individualized Education Program (IEP) in place, the next essential step is to monitor your child's progress throughout the school year. This process ensures that the goals outlined in the IEP are being met and that your child is receiving the appropriate services and supports.

While it's important to feel empowered in your role as a parent, many parents initially struggle with monitoring their child's progress on their own. It's common to feel overwhelmed by the amount of information and the various assessments involved. Recognizing that this can be a complex and emotional process is vital, but with the right tools and strategies, you can confidently navigate it.

Let's explore how to effectively monitor your child's progress, empowering you to stay engaged and informed every step of the way.

Step 1: Understanding Progress Monitoring

Understanding how your child's progress is monitored is the first step in advocating for their needs. The IEP should outline how progress will be measured and reported, but it's essential to dig deeper to ensure you fully grasp the methods used.

Types of Assessments: Familiarize yourself with the different types of assessments that may be used, including formal assessments (like standardized tests) and informal assessments (like observations and work samples). Each type serves a purpose in gauging your child's development.

Frequency of Monitoring: The IEP should specify how often progress will be measured. This could range from quarterly assessments to monthly check-ins. Understanding this timeline will help you stay informed about your child's growth.

One father I worked with initially felt confident in understanding the progress monitoring process but soon found himself confused when it came to the types of assessments being used. After trying to decipher various reports and metrics on his own, he became frustrated and unsure if his son was truly making progress. When he reached out to our team for support, we helped him clarify the assessment methods and frequency outlined in the IEP. This support transformed his understanding and confidence, allowing him to actively engage with the school regarding his son's progress.

Step 2: Keeping Track of Data

As you monitor your child's progress, it's important to maintain organized records of all relevant data. This not only helps you assess growth but also provides a foundation for discussions during IEP meetings.

Create a Progress Log: Start a dedicated progress log where you can record observations, assessments, and any notes from meetings with teachers or specialists. This will be your go to resource for tracking your child's development over time.

Collect Samples of Work: Save examples of your child's work to visually demonstrate their progress. Having tangible evidence can be powerful during discussions with the IEP team.

In one case, a mother attempted to keep track of her child's progress but found herself overwhelmed by the sheer volume of information. Despite her best intentions, she struggled to organize everything effectively. After she reached out to our team, we guided her in creating a streamlined progress log that made it easier to track her child's growth. By utilizing a simple system, she regained her confidence and felt more in control of the monitoring process.

Step 3: Regular Check-ins with Educators

Maintaining open lines of communication with your child's teachers and support staff is critical in monitoring progress. Regular check-ins will help you stay informed about how your child is performing in the classroom and provide opportunities for collaboration.

Schedule Meetings: Request periodic meetings with your child's educators to discuss their progress and any concerns that may arise. These meetings can be brief but will allow you to stay engaged in your child's educational journey.

Ask for Feedback: Don't hesitate to seek feedback from teachers regarding specific goals outlined in the IEP. Ask them to share insights into your child's strengths and areas where they may need additional support.

One parent I worked with initially felt hesitant to

schedule regular check ins with the school. She worried that her questions might seem trivial or that she would be seen as overly involved. However, when she finally took the initiative to schedule meetings, she was pleasantly surprised by the openness of her child's teachers. They welcomed her inquiries and appreciated her commitment to her child's education. This experience not only informed her about her child's progress but also strengthened the relationship between her and the school team.

Step 4: Analyzing Progress Reports

As progress reports come in, it's essential to analyze them critically. Understanding what the data means in relation to your child's goals will help you advocate more effectively.

Look for Patterns: Review progress reports to identify patterns over time. Is your child consistently improving in certain areas, or are there subjects where they seem to struggle? This analysis will provide valuable insights into their learning journey.

Compare with IEP Goals: Cross reference the progress reports with the goals outlined in the IEP. Are the goals being met? If not, consider discussing this during your next meeting with the IEP team.

A father initially felt overwhelmed when he received his child's progress reports. He had high expectations for his son's performance, but the data presented left him feeling confused and discouraged. When he reached out to our team, we helped him analyze the reports and relate them back to the IEP goals. With this newfound clarity, he was able to approach the school with specific questions and concerns, enabling him to advocate more effectively for his son's needs.

Step 5: Adjusting the IEP When Necessary

As you monitor your child's progress, you may notice areas where adjustments to the IEP are necessary. It's crucial to advocate for changes based on your observations and the data collected.

Identify Areas for Improvement: If your child is consistently struggling to meet their goals, it may be time to request a review of the IEP. Document your observations and provide evidence to support your request.

Request an IEP Meeting: If you feel that changes are needed, don't hesitate to request an IEP meeting to discuss your concerns. Prepare in advance by gathering data and formulating your thoughts to present during the meeting.

One mother attempted to manage her child's IEP independently but soon became overwhelmed by the amount of information she was trying to process. After a few months, she realized her child was not making the expected progress. When she reached out for support, we helped her prepare for an IEP meeting to advocate for necessary changes. By organizing her observations and articulating her concerns, she felt empowered to discuss her child's needs. This proactive approach led to significant revisions in the IEP, allowing her child to receive the support required for success.

Conclusion: Your Role as a Continuous Advocate

Monitoring your child's progress is an ongoing responsibility that is vital to ensuring the success of their

IEP. By understanding progress monitoring, keeping track of data, maintaining regular check ins with educators, analyzing reports, and adjusting the IEP as necessary, you can navigate this process with confidence.

While it's natural to feel out of your league at times, remember that your insights and observations are invaluable. You are not alone in this journey—seeking support when needed can help you advocate effectively for your child.

In the next chapter, we will delve into the process of resolving conflicts and navigating disputes within the IEP framework. You will gain strategies for addressing concerns while maintaining a collaborative relationship with the school. Your role as an advocate is critical, and each step you take strengthens your child's educational experience.

7

NAVIGATING CONFLICT AND DISPUTES

As a dedicated advocate for your child, you will undoubtedly face challenges throughout the IEP process. Conflicts and disputes can arise at any stage, whether over the interpretation of assessment results, the provision of services, or the effectiveness of interventions. While these moments can feel daunting, knowing how to navigate them effectively will empower you to continue advocating for your child's needs.

It's natural to feel overwhelmed in these situations, especially when faced with seasoned professionals who may have more experience in the field. Recognizing that conflicts can arise is crucial, but with the right strategies and tools, you can confidently approach these discussions.

Let's explore how to navigate conflicts and disputes effectively, ensuring that your child's educational rights are upheld while fostering a collaborative relationship with the IEP team.\

Step 1: Identifying Potential Areas of Conflict

Understanding where conflicts may arise is the first step in preparing to navigate them. Conflicts can occur for a variety of reasons, including misunderstandings, differing opinions about your child's needs, or disagreements regarding the effectiveness of the IEP. Here are some common areas where disputes may arise:

Service Delivery: Conflicts may arise if you believe your child is not receiving the services outlined in the IEP. Being aware of these discrepancies will allow you to address them proactively.

Assessment Results: Disagreements over assessment outcomes can lead to conflict. It's essential to be prepared to discuss your child's strengths and weaknesses based on these results.

One mother I worked with initially felt confident in discussing her child's needs during IEP meetings. However, she found herself in conflict when her child's teachers reported that the accommodations outlined in the IEP were not being fully implemented. The mother tried to address this issue herself but quickly felt overwhelmed by the technicalities involved. When she reached out to our team, we helped her identify the specific areas of concern and prepare a strategy for addressing them with the school. By acknowledging potential areas of conflict, she was able to approach the situation with greater confidence.

Step 2: Preparing for Difficult Conversations

When preparing to address conflicts, effective communication is key. Here are some strategies to help you prepare for difficult conversations with the IEP team:

Gather Evidence: Before approaching the school, collect relevant documentation to support your concerns. This may include progress reports, assessment results, and notes from previous meetings. Having concrete evidence will strengthen your case and provide clarity.

Practice Your Talking Points: Before the meeting, take time to rehearse your main points. Practicing will not only help you articulate your thoughts more clearly but will also boost your confidence.

A father initially tried to address concerns about his child's lack of progress on his own, but he quickly became overwhelmed by the conversation. He realized he needed to prepare more effectively for the next IEP meeting. After reaching out for support, we helped him gather documentation and rehearse his points. When he returned to the meeting, he was surprised at how much more confident he felt, allowing him to navigate the conversation without feeling intimidated.

Step 3: Using Collaborative Language

As you engage in discussions about conflicts, using collaborative language can help foster a more productive atmosphere. Instead of adopting an adversarial tone, aim to express your concerns in a way that encourages dialogue and collaboration.

Frame Concerns Positively: Instead of saying, "The school is not doing enough for my child," you might say, "I appreciate the efforts the school is making, but I have some concerns about how we can better support my child's needs."

Focus on Solutions: Rather than solely highlighting the problems, be prepared to discuss potential solutions. This demonstrates that you're invested in finding a way forward for your child.

A mother I assisted struggled with feeling confrontational during IEP meetings. She often expressed her concerns but noticed that her tone was perceived as aggressive. With guidance, she learned to reframe her language to promote collaboration. When she approached her next meeting with a solutions focused mindset, the dynamics shifted positively. The IEP team responded more openly, and they worked together to develop a plan that truly supported her child's needs.

Step 4: Knowing When to Escalate

Sometimes, despite your best efforts, conflicts may not resolve at the level of the IEP team. In these cases, it's important to know when to escalate the issue while maintaining professionalism. Here are some steps to consider:

Request a Mediation: If you find that direct conversations are not yielding results, consider requesting mediation. This process involves a neutral third party who can help facilitate discussions and find common ground.

Know Your Rights: Familiarize yourself with your rights as a parent within the special education framework. Understanding the laws and regulations surrounding special education will empower you to advocate more effectively.

One father felt that his concerns about his child's services were falling on deaf ears. Despite numerous discussions with the IEP team, he felt as though they weren't making the necessary changes. After consulting with us, he decided to request a mediation session. We assisted him in preparing his case, and during mediation, he confidently articulated his concerns and the changes he sought. By knowing when to escalate the issue, he was able to advocate successfully for his child's needs.

Step 5: Reflecting on the Experience

After navigating a conflict, take the time to reflect on the experience. This can provide valuable insights and help you prepare for future interactions.

What Worked Well? Consider what strategies were effective during the discussions. Did certain phrases or approaches resonate with the IEP team?

What Can Be Improved? Reflect on any aspects of the conversation that could have gone more smoothly. Identifying these areas can help you refine your approach in the future.

One mother found herself in a challenging situation when discussing her child's IEP. Afterward, she took time to reflect on what had transpired. By analyzing her approach, she realized that while she had effectively communicated her concerns, she could improve her active listening skills. With this newfound awareness, she sought guidance from our team to enhance her communication strategies. This reflection ultimately led to stronger interactions in subsequent meetings, enabling her to advocate even more effectively.

Conclusion: Embracing Challenges as Growth Opportunities

Navigating conflicts and disputes within the IEP process can be challenging, but each experience offers an opportunity for growth. By identifying potential areas of conflict, preparing for difficult conversations, using collaborative language, knowing when to escalate, and reflecting on your experiences, you can navigate these challenges with confidence.

Remember, it's normal to feel out of your league at times, but your dedication to your child's education and wellbeing is invaluable. Seeking support when needed is a strength, not a weakness. As you continue to advocate for your child, you will develop greater resilience and skill in navigating conflicts.

In the next chapter, we will explore the transition process as your child approaches adulthood, discussing how to prepare for this significant milestone. You are well on your way to becoming a seasoned advocate, and each chapter brings you closer to empowering your child for their future

8

NAVIGATING THE IEP MEETING: STRATEGIES FOR SUCCESS

The Individualized Education Program (IEP) meeting is a pivotal moment in your child's educational journey. It's where decisions are made that can shape your child's future, from their learning environment to the supports they receive. Attending this meeting with a sense of confidence and clarity is crucial, yet many parents find it overwhelming due to the complexity of the process and the technical nature of special education language.

While some parents initially try to handle these meetings on their own, it's common to feel lost in the flood of information and unsure about how to advocate effectively. The good news is, you're already taking the right steps by seeking guidance to ensure the best possible outcome for your child.

Step 1: Preparing for the Meeting

Preparation is the cornerstone of success when it comes to navigating an IEP meeting. While it's easy to think you can simply show up and trust the school to take the lead, being prepared helps you stay in control of the conversation.

Review the IEP in Advance: Take time to thoroughly review the draft IEP or the most recent version of the plan. Pay close attention to the goals, accommodations, and services outlined.

Gather Documentation: Collect any relevant documents, such as evaluations, progress reports, and correspondence with teachers. These materials will serve as evidence when advocating for your child's needs.

Create a List of Priorities: Think about your top priorities for your child and write them down. This might include specific goals for their academic growth, social development, or accommodations that you feel are necessary.

One parent I worked with, Jennifer, believed that reviewing the IEP briefly the night before the meeting would be sufficient. However, as the meeting progressed, she realized she hadn't fully understood certain technical terms, and key points were glossed over without discussion. Feeling overwhelmed and unsure of how to proceed, Jennifer decided to seek our support for the next meeting. Together, we worked through the IEP line by line, clarifying the language and identifying areas for improvement. With this preparation, Jennifer walked into the next meeting confident and informed, securing the necessary supports for her child.

Step 2: Understanding Your Rights and the School's Responsibilities

Understanding your rights as a parent in the IEP process is essential. Many parents assume the school will automatically act in their child's best interest, but knowing the school's responsibilities and your legal rights as an advocate will give you an edge in the meeting.

Know the Law: Familiarize yourself with the Individuals with Disabilities Education Act (IDEA). This law ensures that your child is entitled to a free and appropriate public education, tailored to their unique needs.

Request Clarifications: If you don't understand something during the meeting, don't hesitate to ask for clarification. The IEP process can be filled with jargon, but it's important that you fully understand what's being discussed.

Ask for Data: Ensure that all decisions made about your child's education are backed by data. This includes evaluation results, progress reports, and any relevant assessments.

One father, Michael, was well-intentioned but found himself lost in the legal jargon during his first few IEP meetings. He believed he understood the basics but often left meetings feeling uncertain about what had been agreed upon. After multiple meetings where services were either delayed or inadequately explained, Michael reached out to us for support. We explained his rights under IDEA and coached him through the process, equipping him with the right questions to ask. At the next meeting, he confidently requested data to support the school's recommendations, and the meeting became more productive and transparent.

Step 3: Managing Emotions During the Meeting

Attending an IEP meeting can be an emotional experience. It's natural to feel passionate about your child's needs and their future, but managing your emotions in the meeting will help you advocate more effectively.

Stay Focused on the Facts: While it's okay to express concern, focusing on objective facts and data will make your arguments more compelling. Use the documentation you've prepared to support your points.

Use Active Listening: It's easy to get caught up in formulating your next response, but active listening is crucial in understanding the school's perspective. Take notes and clarify any points you don't understand.

Take Breaks if Needed: If emotions are running high or if you feel overwhelmed, don't hesitate to request a short break. Regrouping for a few minutes can help you stay calm and collected.

I remember working with a parent named Sarah, who came to her first few meetings with strong emotions. She was understandably frustrated by her child's lack of progress and felt that the school wasn't doing enough. Unfortunately, these meetings often ended with heightened emotions and little resolution. We worked together to channel her passion into preparation. By focusing on the data and taking breaks when needed, Sarah was able to express her concerns in a calm and assertive way. The result was a more productive conversation that led to immediate improvements in her child's services.

Step 4: Engaging as an Equal Team Member

One of the most critical aspects of the IEP meeting is remembering that you are an equal member of the IEP team. While the school staff may be the "experts" in education, you are the expert on your child. Your insights and input are invaluable.

Speak Up: Don't be afraid to voice your concerns, ask questions, or offer suggestions. Your input is critical to developing an IEP that truly meets your child's needs.

Collaborate, Don't Confront: While it's important to advocate assertively, maintaining a collaborative tone will often lead to better outcomes. Frame your concerns as a desire to work together for your child's success.

Clarify Agreements: Before the meeting ends, make sure you have a clear understanding of what has been agreed upon. Confirm timelines, next steps, and responsibilities.

One parent, David, felt initially out of place in the IEP meetings, thinking the school knew best. As a result, he hesitated to offer his opinions or challenge the school's recommendations. After a particularly frustrating meeting where he felt his concerns were brushed aside, David enlisted our help. We empowered him with tools to engage in the process as an equal team member. By asserting his role and participating more actively, David was able to advocate for meaningful changes that directly benefited his child's learning experience.

Step 5: When to Seek Professional Support

Despite your best efforts, there may come a time when handling the IEP process on your own becomes too overwhelming. Knowing when to seek professional support is a sign of strength, not weakness. Whether it's the technicalities of the IEP, communication breakdowns with the school, or concerns about legal rights, a knowledgeable advocate can make a significant difference.

Consider an Advocate or Attorney: If you're facing significant challenges, consider bringing in an advocate or special education attorney to help guide you through the process. Their expertise can ease your burden and ensure that your child receives the support they deserve.

Recognize the Red Flags: If you notice that the school isn't following through on agreements, isn't providing data to support their decisions, or is delaying services, it may be time to seek outside help.

IEPs Made Easy: A Parent's Step-by-Step Guide to Special Education Advocacy

I worked with a family who had initially tried to manage everything themselves. The parents were dedicated and had done their research, but as the meetings grew more contentious and the school started to push back on services, they realized they needed assistance. Once we stepped in, we helped refocus the meetings on their child's needs, brought in data that the school had previously overlooked, and secured additional services that had been denied. Their child's progress improved dramatically as a result.

Conclusion: Empowered Advocacy, Supported Advocacy

Attending an IEP meeting on your own can be a daunting task, but preparation, knowledge of your rights, and emotional composure can go a long way in ensuring a successful outcome for your child. You've already made significant strides by understanding the importance of advocacy, and you now have the tools to make your voice heard in these meetings.

However, if the process becomes overwhelming or if you feel the school isn't fully addressing your child's needs, it's okay to seek additional support. Remember, true advocacy doesn't mean doing it alone—it means ensuring that your child gets what they need, by whatever means necessary.

Your child's success is the ultimate goal, and with the right tools, team, and strategies, you can ensure they receive the education and support they deserve.

9

THE IMPORTANCE OF ONGOING ADVOCACY AND SUPPORT

As your child transitions into adulthood, the need for advocacy does not diminish; it evolves. The journey of ensuring your child receives the necessary support and services continues even after high school. This chapter focuses on the importance of ongoing advocacy, the role of support systems, and how you can navigate this critical phase with confidence.

You may find that the postsecondary landscape can feel like uncharted territory. It's not uncommon for parents to feel out of their league when transitioning their child into adulthood. Recognizing that this is a normal feeling is the first step toward empowerment. Many parents have faced similar challenges and sought guidance, which can make a significant difference in navigating this new chapter of life.

Step 1: Understanding the Shift in Advocacy

As your child transitions to adulthood, the nature of advocacy shifts from primarily focusing on educational rights to broader life skills and independence. Understanding this shift will help you better navigate the new landscape:

Embrace the Change: While you may have felt confident advocating for your child in the school system, the postsecondary world presents different challenges. It's important to embrace this change and recognize that your role as an advocate is still crucial.

Focus on Self Advocacy: Encourage your child to take on more responsibility for their advocacy. Teaching them to articulate their needs and preferences is an invaluable skill that will serve them throughout their life.

A mother I assisted initially felt overwhelmed when her child graduated high school. She had spent years navigating the IEP process and suddenly found herself unsure of how to advocate effectively in a new environment. After we discussed the importance of fostering her child's self advocacy skills, she began to see her child in a different light. By helping her child take the lead in conversations about their needs, she realized her role was evolving rather than diminishing.

Step 2: Building a Support Network

Establishing a robust support network is essential for ongoing advocacy. This network can provide guidance, resources, and a sense of community. Here's how to build that network:

Connect with Other Parents: Joining support groups or networks for parents of children with disabilities can provide valuable insights and encouragement. Sharing experiences with others can help you feel less isolated and more empowered.

Seek Professional Guidance: As your child transitions into adulthood, professional advocates or consultants can offer expert advice on navigating the complexities of postsecondary education, employment, and independent living.

A father initially believed he could handle everything on his own. However, as he faced challenges in securing support for his child, he became overwhelmed. It wasn't until he reached out to a local support group that he discovered the wealth of knowledge and resources available. Through shared experiences and collective problem solving, he gained valuable insights that not only assisted him but also bolstered his confidence in advocating for his child.

Step 3: Staying Informed About Rights and Resources

As your child transitions into adulthood, it's crucial to stay informed about their rights and available resources. This knowledge will empower you to advocate effectively on their behalf:

Familiarize Yourself with Adult Services: Research the services and supports available for adults with disabilities, such as vocational rehabilitation programs, community resources, and government assistance.

Understand Legal Protections: Knowing your child's rights under the Americans with Disabilities Act (ADA) and other relevant legislation is essential for effective advocacy. This knowledge allows you to ensure that your child receives the accommodations and support they need in various settings.

One mother thought she could navigate the adult service landscape without additional help. As she attempted to secure resources for her child, she quickly felt overwhelmed by the complexity of the system. After seeking our assistance, she learned about various adult services available in her community. With this newfound knowledge, she felt empowered to advocate for her child's needs and secure the necessary supports.

Step 4: Navigating Employment Opportunities

Finding meaningful employment is a key aspect of your child's transition to adulthood. Ongoing advocacy in this area is crucial to ensure that your child has access to suitable job opportunities:

Explore Vocational Training Programs: Research vocational programs that align with your child's interests and strengths. Many programs offer specialized training designed for individuals with disabilities.

Promote Self Advocacy in Job Settings: Encourage your child to advocate for themselves in the workplace. This might involve discussing accommodations, requesting support, or communicating their preferences and strengths to employers.

A father initially believed he could help his child secure a job without any outside support. However, he quickly realized the job search process was more complex than he anticipated. After enlisting our help, we guided him in researching suitable job opportunities and preparing his child for interviews. This support not only alleviated his stress but also empowered his child to take an active role in their job search, leading to a successful employment outcome.

Step 5: Celebrating Achievements and Progress

As your child navigates adulthood, celebrating their achievements, no matter how small, is essential. Acknowledging progress fosters a sense of accomplishment and motivates both you and your child:

Recognize Milestones: Whether it's completing a vocational program, securing a job, or developing essential life skills, celebrating these milestones reinforces your child's growth and independence.

Create a Positive Narrative: Focus on your child's strengths and successes, even in the face of challenges. A positive narrative encourages resilience and reinforces their ability to advocate for themselves.

A mother initially felt daunted by the idea of celebrating her child's achievements. She often downplayed successes, believing they were not significant enough to warrant recognition. After discussing the importance of celebrating progress, she began to acknowledge her child's milestones. This shift in perspective not only strengthened their bond but also motivated her child to continue striving for success in their endeavors.

Conclusion: Embracing Your Role as an Ongoing Advocate

As your child transitions into adulthood, the journey of advocacy continues. By understanding the shift in advocacy, building a support network, staying informed about rights and resources, navigating employment opportunities, and celebrating achievements, you are preparing to advocate effectively for your child's needs.

While the landscape may feel unfamiliar at times, your commitment to your child's success is unwavering. Remember, seeking assistance and support is a sign of strength, not weakness. As you continue this journey, embrace the challenges as opportunities for growth and empowerment—for both you and your child.

In the next chapter, we will explore strategies for fostering independence and self sufficiency as your child navigates adulthood. Your advocacy journey is far from over, and each step brings you closer to empowering your child to thrive in their future.

10

FOSTERING INDEPENDENCE AND SELFSUFFICIENCY

As your child embarks on adulthood, fostering independence and self sufficiency becomes a cornerstone of their growth. This chapter will explore practical strategies for encouraging independence while recognizing the challenges that may arise along the way. Your role as a parent is essential, and while you may feel equipped to guide your child, it's important to acknowledge that the journey can sometimes feel overwhelming. You are not alone; many parents face similar challenges and have sought support to navigate this critical phase.

Encouraging independence means empowering your child to take charge of their life, make decisions, and learn essential skills. While it's natural to worry about their ability to thrive independently, believing in their potential is a powerful tool that can lead to success.

Step 1: Identifying Life Skills for Independence

The first step in fostering independence is to identify the key life skills your child needs to master. Understanding which skills to focus on will create a solid foundation for their self sufficiency:

Assess Individual Needs: Consider your child's strengths and areas for improvement. Skills such as personal finance, selfcare, household management, and social skills are crucial for living independently.

Set Realistic Goals: Collaborate with your child to set achievable goals in these areas. Breaking down each skill into manageable steps can make the learning process feel less overwhelming.

A mother I worked with initially felt hesitant about allowing her child to handle daily tasks. She believed her child wasn't ready for such responsibilities and was concerned about the potential for mistakes. However, when she sought our guidance, we encouraged her to assess her child's capabilities and set realistic goals. With this shift in perspective, she began allowing her child to take on small tasks. Over time, she witnessed her child's confidence grow as they developed essential life **skills.**

Step 2: Creating a Supportive Learning Environment

Your home can serve as an excellent training ground for independence. Creating a supportive learning environment is vital for helping your child practice and develop essential life skills:

Encourage Participation: Involve your child in daily household activities. This may include meal planning, grocery shopping, or budgeting. By participating in these tasks, they gain valuable hands on experience.

Offer Guidance, Not Control: While it's important to provide support, it's equally vital to step back and allow your child to make decisions and learn from their experiences. Offering guidance rather than control fosters a sense of ownership.

One father initially attempted to manage all household tasks, believing he was protecting his child from making mistakes. However, he soon realized this approach hindered his child's growth. After consulting with us, he learned to offer guidance while allowing his child to take the lead. This transition not only empowered his child but also lightened the father's load, creating a more balanced approach to independence.

Step 3: Teaching Problem Solving Skills

Encouraging independence also involves equipping your child with problem solving skills. This enables them to navigate challenges effectively and build confidence in their abilities:

Encourage Critical Thinking: When faced with a challenge, ask your child questions that prompt them to think critically about potential solutions. This helps them develop problem solving strategies.

Role Playing Scenarios: Engage in roleplaying exercises to simulate real life situations your child may encounter. This practice can prepare them to handle challenges with confidence.

A mother attempted to solve her child's problems for them, believing this was the best way to support them. However, she soon found that her child was hesitant to make decisions independently. When she sought our assistance, we guided her in encouraging critical thinking and problem solving. By stepping back and allowing her child to tackle challenges, she saw remarkable growth in their confidence and ability to navigate difficulties on their own.

Step 4: Supporting Social Skills Development

Social skills play a vital role in fostering independence. Building strong interpersonal skills will enable your child to form connections and navigate various social situations:

Practice Social Interactions: Encourage your child to engage in social activities and practice interactions with peers. This might include joining clubs, participating in community events, or volunteering.

Model Appropriate Behaviors: As a parent, model positive social behaviors and communication skills. Your child will learn from observing your interactions with others.

A father found it challenging to encourage his child to socialize, fearing they would face rejection or difficulty connecting with peers. After consulting with us, he realized the importance of gradual exposure to social situations. By starting with small, low pressure interactions, he helped his child build confidence and develop essential social skills over time.

Step 5: Encouraging Financial Literacy

Financial literacy is a crucial aspect of independence. Teaching your child about budgeting, saving, and responsible spending will empower them to manage their finances effectively:

Create a Budget Together: Work with your child to create a budget that outlines their income, expenses, and savings goals. This hands on approach can foster a sense of responsibility.

Discuss Money Management Strategies: Teach your child

about saving, spending wisely, and making informed financial decisions. Providing them with real life scenarios can enhance their understanding.

A mother initially believed her child was too young to learn about financial management. However, when she sought assistance, we emphasized the importance of teaching these skills early on. By gradually introducing financial concepts, she empowered her child to take charge of their finances, instilling confidence in their ability to navigate financial responsibilities.

Step 6: Celebrating Independence Milestones

As your child progresses on their journey toward independence, celebrating their achievements is essential. Recognizing milestones reinforces their efforts and motivates them to continue striving for growth:

Acknowledge Achievements: Celebrate even the small victories, whether it's mastering a life skill, completing a task, or making a responsible decision. Positive reinforcement builds confidence.

Create a Ritual for Celebration: Establish a family tradition for celebrating milestones, such as a special dinner or a small gift. This creates a sense of accomplishment and encourages your child to continue developing their skills.

A father initially downplayed his child's achievements, believing that only major milestones warranted celebration. After seeking our guidance, he learned the importance of acknowledging progress along the way. By implementing a family ritual for celebrating milestones, he fostered a sense of pride in his child, reinforcing their confidence in pursuing independence.

Conclusion: Embracing the Path to Independence

Fostering independence and self sufficiency in your child is a gradual process that requires patience, understanding, and encouragement. By identifying life skills, creating a supportive learning environment, teaching problem solving skills, supporting social skills development, encouraging financial literacy, and celebrating achievements, you are equipping your child for a successful future.

While the journey toward independence can feel overwhelming at times, your commitment to your child's growth is invaluable. Embrace the challenges as opportunities for learning and development—for both you and your child. You are not alone in this endeavor, and seeking support is a sign of strength.

As we conclude this guide, remember that advocacy does not end here; it is an ongoing journey that continues to evolve. Your role as an advocate, parent, and supporter is vital in ensuring your child thrives in adulthood. Each step you take fosters confidence and independence, empowering your child to embrace their future with resilience and determination.

11

PREPARING FOR LIFE AFTER HIGH SCHOOL

As your child approaches the transition out of high school, the journey toward adulthood takes on new dimensions. This chapter focuses on preparing for life after high school, ensuring that your child has the necessary tools and resources to thrive in this next phase. While the prospect of this transition can be daunting, it's crucial to remember that you are not alone—many parents face similar challenges, and support is available.

The transition from high school can evoke a range of emotions, from excitement about newfound freedom to anxiety about the unknown. It's normal to feel both hopeful and apprehensive. Recognizing these feelings is the first step in building confidence—for you and your child.

Step 1: Understanding Transition Planning

Transition planning is a critical component of preparing your child for life after high school. It involves mapping out a plan that addresses their individual needs, preferences, and goals:

Start Early: The process of transition planning should begin well before graduation. Engaging in discussions about your child's aspirations and interests in their junior year can set the foundation for a successful transition.

Collaborate with the IEP Team: Ensure that your child's Individualized Education Program (IEP) includes a transition plan that outlines specific goals and services designed to support their postsecondary journey.

A mother I assisted initially thought she could handle the transition planning process independently. However, as graduation approached, she realized the complexity of the process was overwhelming. After seeking our guidance, we collaborated with the IEP team to create a comprehensive transition plan. This collaboration not only alleviated her stress but also instilled confidence in her ability to navigate the process effectively.

Step 2: Exploring Postsecondary Options

The postsecondary landscape offers a variety of opportunities, including vocational training, community college, or traditional university paths. Understanding these options is crucial for making informed decisions:

Research Programs: Encourage your child to explore different postsecondary programs that align with their interests and strengths. Each option offers unique experiences and learning environments.

Visit Campuses: Touring campuses or vocational training centers can help your child visualize their future and determine what environment feels right for them.

One father initially believed his child was solely interested in a traditional college experience. However, as he explored other options, he realized that vocational training could be a better fit. After we assisted him in researching various programs, he and his child visited a local trade school. This experience opened their eyes to new possibilities and options that aligned more closely with his child's interests and strengths.

Step 3: Building a Support System

A strong support system is essential for navigating the challenges of life after high school. Building connections can provide guidance and encouragement as your child embarks on this journey:

Connect with Peer Support Groups: Encourage your child to join support groups or networks for young adults with disabilities. These connections can foster friendships and provide valuable insights.

Engage with Community Resources: Many communities offer resources specifically designed to support young adults with disabilities in their transition. Research local organizations and programs that can assist your child.

A mother initially tried to manage her child's transition on her own, believing she could provide all the support needed. However, as the challenges grew, she found herself feeling overwhelmed. After reaching out for help, she discovered local support groups that connected her child with peers facing similar transitions. This newfound community not only alleviated her stress but also provided her child with a sense of belonging and understanding.

Step 4: Developing Life Skills

Life skills are fundamental for your child's success in adulthood. Focusing on essential skills will empower them to navigate daily life more independently:

Encourage Practical Skills: Involve your child in everyday tasks such as cooking, cleaning, and budgeting. Teaching them these skills fosters independence and confidence.

Create a Life Skills Curriculum: Develop a plan that outlines the specific life skills your child needs to learn and incorporate them into your daily routine.

A father initially underestimated the importance of teaching life skills to his child. He believed they would naturally develop these skills over time. However, when he observed his child struggling with daily tasks, he realized the need for a structured approach. After we collaborated on a life skills curriculum, he began to see significant progress. His child developed newfound confidence in their ability to handle everyday responsibilities.

Step 5: Navigating Employment Opportunities

Employment is a crucial aspect of independence. Supporting your child in finding meaningful work will help them build confidence and self sufficiency:

Explore Vocational Training: Encourage your child to participate in vocational training programs that align with their interests and career goals. These programs can provide valuable skills and certifications.

Practice Interviewing Skills: Conduct mock interviews with your child to help them feel more comfortable in real job interviews. This practice can enhance their confidence and preparedness.

A mother thought her child was ready to enter the job market without any formal preparation. However, when they faced challenges during interviews, she realized the need for additional support. After seeking our assistance, we helped her child practice interviewing skills. This preparation led to increased confidence and ultimately resulted in a successful job placement.

Step 6: Emphasizing Self-Advocacy

Encouraging your child to advocate for themselves is essential for their growth and independence. Developing self advocacy skills enables them to express their needs and preferences effectively:

Teach Communication Skills: Roleplay various scenarios where your child may need to advocate for themselves, such as discussing accommodations in college or at work.

Empower Decision Making: Encourage your child to make decisions about their future, whether it's related to education, employment, or social activities. This empowerment fosters a sense of ownership.

A father initially struggled with the idea of letting his child advocate for themselves. He believed that protecting them from potential challenges was his responsibility. However, after seeking our guidance, he learned the importance of self advocacy. By allowing his child to voice their opinions and preferences, he witnessed their confidence flourish as they began to navigate various situations independently.

Step 7: Celebrating Achievements and Milestones

Create a Tradition of Celebration: Establish a family tradition for recognizing achievements, such as a special dinner or a small gift. This creates a positive atmosphere around milestones.

A mother initially felt that only significant achievements warranted celebration. After consulting with us, she recognized the importance of acknowledging small victories as well. By implementing a family tradition of celebrating accomplishments, she fostered a sense of pride in her child, motivating them to continue striving for growth and independence.

Conclusion: Embracing the Transition to Adulthood

Preparing for life after high school is a significant milestone in your child's journey toward independence. By understanding transition planning, exploring postsecondary options, building a support system, developing life skills, navigating employment opportunities, emphasizing self-advocacy, and celebrating achievements, you are equipping your child for a successful future.

While the path to independence can feel daunting at times, your unwavering commitment to your child's growth is invaluable. Embrace the challenges as opportunities for learning and development—for both you and your child. Remember that seeking assistance and support is a sign of strength. As you continue this journey, recognize that your role as an advocate, parent, and supporter is vital in ensuring your child thrives as they step into adulthood. Each step you take fosters confidence and independence, empowering your child to embrace their future with resilience and determination. The journey may be complex, but together, you will navigate it successfully.

ABOUT THE AUTHOR

LeTonya F. Moore, Esq. is a passionate advocate and award-winning attorney specializing in special education law and international business. As a mother and seasoned lawyer, LeTonya deeply understands the challenges parents face when navigating the complex special education system. With decades of experience representing families, she empowers parents to take control of their child's educational future. Through her bestselling book, *IEPs Made Easy: A Parent's Step-by-Step Guide to Special Education Advocacy*, she simplifies the process and gives parents the tools they need to advocate effectively. Her commitment to ensuring every child receives the education they deserve has earned her the trust of countless families. By choosing LeTonya as your advocate, you are not just hiring a legal expert, but a partner who will stand with you, passionately fighting for your child's rights every step of the way. Learn more at edlawadvocates.com.

www.ingramcontent.com/pod-product-compliance
Lightning Source LLC
Chambersburg PA
CBHW051948160426
43198CB00013B/2353